Mum, Pip and Tim plan to visit Nan.
They look at the rain.

"Can we go and see Nan soon?" moans Pip.

"No," Mum tells Pip. "We will get wet
feet if we go in the rain!"

"Can we go on the train soon?" moans Tim.

"Not in the rain," sighs Mum. "Go and get a book!"

Pip and Tim look and wait ... and wait ... and wait. "The rain is a pain," moan Tim and Pip. They are fed up.

Pip has a plan. "Get a rain coat and boots," she tells Tim.

Pip and Tim zip and zoom in the rain.

They are soaking wet!

"Rain is fun!" they tell Mum.
"Will it rain at Nan's?"

Spelling and writing

Cover the words below. Say the first word (*wait*). Ask the child to repeat the word and tap out the phonemes in order with his or her fingers, saying each phoneme (*w-ai-t*) and then writing the graphemes to spell the word. Repeat this with the other words.

wait   feet

moan   sigh

book

Understanding the story   Ask the questions below to make sure that the children understand the story.

1 Where are Mum, Pip and Tim planning to go? (page 1)

2 What does Mum tell Tim to do? (page 5)

3 What is Pip's plan? (page 7)

Assessment

Say the phonemes

Point to each grapheme in turn and ask the child to say the corresponding phoneme. Note whether the child is correct each time and go back to any incorrect ones. For *oo*, accept short *oo* (*look*) or long *oo* (*moon*).

Next, cover the graphemes. Say a phoneme and ask the child to write the corresponding grapheme. Practise any that are incorrect.

ai	igh	ee	sh
oo	oa	ng	th

Read the words

Ask the child to sound out a word and then blend the phonemes and say the word. Repeat this with the other words.

high   boat   sheep
boots   train